AF482077

Air Fryer Cookbook for Two

Easy and Delicious Air Fryer Recipes for You and Your Partner

Melanie Bennet

for clarifying purposes only and are owned by the owners themselves, not affiliated with this document.

Table of Contents

CHAPTER SEVEN

CHAPTER EIGHT

CHAPTER NINE

Dessert **83**

Conclusion **93**

x

Introduction

When you have Gordon Ramsey promoting the air fryer and Oprah Winfrey recommending it, you know it's a good idea to try this trendy new appliance. Whether you have already bought a shiny new air fryer or are still wondering if air fried food tastes good, this book has all the answers.

Using superheated air instead of oil, an air fryer prepares crispy, tender, and delicious foods with fewer calories. The hot air prepares food quickly, so it saves you time. This makes the air fryer an ideal and convenient cooking device for two people.

Taking you into the depths of the world of air frying and providing you with step-by-step guidance to preparing yummy delights effortlessly, this cookbook will make you want to start cooking with an air fryer right away. This book is a must-have for everyone who likes the taste and texture of fried foods.

Whether you are cooking for yourself, a guest, or a loved one, this book offers more than eighty healthy and crunchy ideas you'll want to try. And the best part? Even novice cooks can master these delights.

CHAPTER ONE

Cooking with the Air Fryer

We all know that greasy and deep-fried food is bad for our health. It raises our cholesterol levels, increases our blood pressure, and don't get me started on how badly it affects our weight. You know it, I know it, and yet, when we have crunchy deep-fried chicken in front of us, we just cannot resist the temptation. But what if I tell you that fried food doesn't have to be a guilty pleasure but a healthy satisfaction? What if I tell you that the technology has progressed to the point where you can fry your foods without having to drown them in oil and unhealthy fats?

Meet the air fryer—the revolutionary kitchen appliance that will change how you prepare your foods. An air fryer uses Rapid Air technology to cook foods with little oil. Foods are placed in the fryer's basket, and hot air is circulated rapidly around the ingredients. The air helps heat the food from all sides at once, which is exactly what happens when you deep fry foods using oil. The air fryer uses 90 percent less oil and won't leave your kitchen with a greasy smell. This technology also ensures an optimal temperature is maintained within the fryer to avoid burning your food. The air fryer will make your food crispy on the outside and tender and tasty on the inside!

Benefits of Air Fryers

When you look at a new kitchen appliance, you want to know the benefits of using it before splurging on the purchase. Let's look at a few benefits of the air fryer, which may give you a clearer idea of whether you should consider getting it for your kitchen.

Air Fryer Helps You Cook Healthier

It's hard to deny that fried food tastes good. We all love it. The air fryer lets you enjoy that decadent fried taste with only a spoonful of oil. You'll save calories, lose weight, and get healthier while enjoying crispy French fries and fried chicken. The tray below the air fryer collects all the excess fat that would typically end up in your body when using traditional frying methods.

Air Fryer Saves You Time

Probably the most convenient thing about using an air fryer, this appliance is super time efficient. If you are a busy person (and who isn't nowadays?) and hate coming home just to spend your evening whisking in front of the stove, you will greatly appreciate having this appliance in your kitchen. But that's not all. Besides the fact that the air fryer can prepare delicious meals in a matter of minutes, what's even more amazing is how quickly it is to start cooking. Instead of waiting for a large amount of oil to heat up in the deep fryer, the air fryer can reach a temperature higher than 300 degrees F in an instant.

Air Fryer is an All-in-One Appliance

In addition to fried foods, you can grill, roast, and bake in an air fryer. You can prepare anything from Kentucky fried drumsticks to muffins, roasted veggies, and cakes. There is no need for other pans and pots because, with your air fryer, you will have everything you need to cook restaurant-grade meals.

Air Fryer is Easy to Clean

With an air fryer, there is no need for degreasing and scrubbing the sticky pots and pans after frying with oil. All parts are easily removable and can be washed in the dishwasher, which is convenient. Not to mention, switching to air frying means no more splatters all over your stove. I don't know about you, but I find that a huge plus.

How to Cook in the Air Fryer?

The air fryer is straightforward to use. The instruction in the manual will teach you how to turn it on and off and how to set the cooking time, which is not rocket science since the buttons on the appliance pretty much explain everything.

The air fryer can be used to cook almost everything (except soups which are not recommended), whether fresh or frozen foods. It comes with a few removable parts:

Cooking Basket – you can cook anything inside the cooking basket as it is perfect for frying and baking. The basket comes with lids, which will help increase the cooking speed and keep the splattering inside.

Nonstick Grill Pan – To add an extra smoky flavor and cook your food with the fancy grill marks, you don't have to turn on your actual grill. Just place the grill pan inside the air fryer.

Nonstick Baking Pan – Use the baking pan for anything you wish to bake, from eggs to cakes.

Double Layer Rack – If you need to cook more food, the double rack will help you increase the surface for cooking. Besides, it is also great for burgers and chicken.

Here are the steps to use an air fryer:

1. Place your air fryer on a heat-resistant surface and plug it into a power outlet.

2. Turn it on and set the cooking temperature. Press the START button and allow about 2-3 minutes for preheating.

3. Set the cooking time again and pull out the cooking basket or pan with mittens (Be careful! It will be hot).

4. Place the food inside and add the basket or pan back to the air fryer.

5. Close the lid and let the Air Fryer do its job. When the cooking is done, your air fryer will let you know. Enjoy!

Cooking Times

The following is a cooking chart for some common ingredients to cook in the air fryer. Note that the cooking time increases with larger amounts and may vary with different models of air fryers.

Ingredients	Time	Temperature
Frozen French Fries	14 – 18 minutes	400 degrees F
Frozen Onion Ring	8 – 10 minutes	400 degrees F
Spring Rolls	8 – 15 minutes	360 degrees F
Chicken Wings	20 – 25 minutes	400 degrees F
Chicken Drumsticks	20 – 25 minutes	375 degrees F
Chicken Breasts, Boneless	12 – 15 minutes	380 degrees F
Burgers	15 – 20 minutes	370 degrees F
Steaks	15 – 20 minutes	400 degrees F
Pork Chops	12 – 14 minutes	400 degrees F
Fish Fillets	10 – 15 minutes	400 degrees F
Broccoli	6 minutes	400 degrees F
Carrots	15 minutes	380 degrees F
Cauliflower	12 – 15 minutes	400 degrees F
Green Peppers	15 minutes	400 degrees F
Mushrooms	5 minutes	400 degrees F
Potato Wedges	12 – 15 minutes	400 degrees F
Bread	10 – 20 minutes	360 degrees F
Muffins	10 – 15 minutes	320 degrees F

Tips for Air Frying

Want to become a pro at air frying? Make sure to take advantage of the tips below to set your dinner table with meals that are fried to perfection.

Use a Cooking Spray

Although the air fryer manual says you don't need to add oil, you may still need oil to cook some foods, such as French fries. Otherwise, your food may stick to the fryer's surface. You can spray your air fryer with cooking oil or coat the food slightly with oil. Spraying the fryer with oil is usually more efficient than coating the food with oil. Why? Because this way you will use less oil, but cover much more surface.

Do not Overcrowd the Air Fryer

It may be tempting to cook more food at once and have plenty of leftovers. However, remember that jam-packing your air fryer will lead to undercooked food, as the air doesn't have enough room to circulate.

Shake and Mix

When you cook using oil, the oil helps to mix your food properly, which cooks every little piece in the skillet or pan on all sides. This does not happen in an air fryer since the air is not strong enough to separate the ingredients. To avoid undercooked food, you must open the machine at least once to shake the ingredients in the cooking basket. Most people remove the basket halfway through the cooking to shake the ingredients. For example, if you set a timer for 20 minutes, you would need to pause the fryer after 10 minutes and mix the ingredients before you restart the fryer again.

Check Your Food

Another great thing about the air fryer is that you can open the lid and check your food without disrupting the cooking process. Just like you open your oven to see whether your food is cooked to perfection, you can do the same with the air fryer.

Make an Aluminum Sling

One thing I find challenging about this appliance is getting the cooked food out of it. To make your cooking process a lot easier, make an aluminum sling and put it underneath the baking pan. I suggest a sling that is 24 inches long and 2 inches wide. Now, when cooking is done, you can easily lift your pan with the help of this sling.

Add Some Water

Sometimes, especially when cooking super fatty ingredients (think bacon), the grease inside the Air Fryer can start smoking. This is normal and nothing to worry about; however, if you want to avoid this, I suggest adding just a bit of water underneath the basket.

Start with Room Temperature

When you cook using fresh ingredients, do not start cooking them immediately after taking them out of the fridge. Let the ingredients warm to room temperature before placing them in the fryer. This will reduce the cooking time and will also give you crispier results.

Do More with It

Although this appliance is called an air "fryer," it does a lot more than just frying food. You can make anything from noodles to a pizza in an air fryer. An air fryer has more in common with a fan-forced oven than a deep fryer. You can roast, bake, and grill in an air fryer. In other words, experiment!

Take Good Care of Your Air Fryer

To take good care of your air fryer, you don't have to clean it constantly, but like every other electronic appliance, it does need a certain level of care. If you use your air fryer regularly, you will need to clean it every five to ten days to prevent unwanted smells. Use a dishwasher to clean the removable parts of the fryer or soak them in soapy water before cleaning them gently with a sponge.

CHAPTER TWO

Breakfast Recipes

Vanilla and Cinnamon Toast

Yield: 2 servings
Total Time: 20 minutes
Ingredients:
4 bread slices
2 tablespoons sugar
½ teaspoon cinnamon
¼ teaspoon vanilla extract
2 tablespoons butter, softened

Directions:
1. Set your air fryer to 400 degrees F.
2. Place the sugar, cinnamon, vanilla extract, and butter in a bowl. Stir the mixture until well combined.
3. Brush the cinnamon butter all over the bread slices.
4. Arrange the bread slices in the air fryer. Cook for 5 minutes.
5. Transfer the toasts to a plate.
6. Cut diagonally and top with your favorite toppings.
7. Serve and enjoy!

Easy Egg Potato Hash

Yield: 2 servings
Total Time: 20 minutes
Ingredients:
3 eggs
¼ teaspoon garlic powder
¼ teaspoon paprika
Pinch of nutmeg
Salt and pepper to taste
1 cup flour
1 large potato, peeled and grated

Directions:
1. Set your air fryer to 390 degrees F.
2. In a bowl, beat the eggs along with the spices.
3. Season with salt and pepper to taste, and whisk in the flour.
4. Fold in the shredded potato and then shape the mixture into patties.
5. Spray the bottom of the air fryer with some cooking spray, and arrange the patties inside.
6. Bake for 15 minutes.
7. Serve and enjoy!

Green Omelet

Yield: 2 servings
Total Time: 15 minutes
Ingredients:
4 eggs
Pinch of pepper
Pinch of paprika
¼ teaspoon garlic salt
¼ cup chopped spinach
2 tablespoons chopped kale
A handful of basil, chopped
1 tablespoon heavy cream
2 tablespoons grated parmesan cheese

Directions:
1. Preheat your air fryer to 330 degrees F.
2. In a bowl, beat the eggs with the spices and salt.
3. Stir in the greens, cream, and parmesan cheese.
4. Place a small pan inside the air fryer and spray with a non-stick cooking spray.
5. Pour the egg mixture into the pan.
6. Bake the omelet for 10 minutes.
7. Serve and enjoy!

Soufflé

Yield: 2 servings
Total Time: 10 minutes
Ingredients:
2 eggs, beaten
2 tablespoons cream
1 tablespoon red pepper flakes
1 tablespoon fresh parsley

Directions:
1. Preheat the air fryer to 400 degrees F.
2. In a bowl, combine eggs with cream, red pepper flakes, and parsley. Pour into two soufflé cups and set in the air fryer.
3. Cook for 5 minutes if you want soft eggs and 8 minutes if you prefer hard eggs.

Bacon and Cheese Egg Cups

Yield: 2 servings
Total Time: 20 minutes
Ingredients:
4 tomato slices
2 bread slices
2 bacon slices, chopped
2 tablespoons grated parmesan cheese
¼ teaspoon maple syrup
¼ teaspoon balsamic vinegar
2 eggs
Salt and pepper to taste

Directions:
1. Preheat your air fryer to 320 degrees F.
2. Spray two large ramekins with some cooking spray.
3. Place the bread slices at the bottom of the ramekins.
4. Top each bread slice with two tomato slices and bacon.
5. Crack the eggs over the tomatoes and sprinkle with the cheese.
6. Drizzle the balsamic vinegar and maple syrup over and then season with salt and pepper, to taste.
7. Place the ramekins in the air fryer and bake for 10 minutes.
8. Serve and enjoy!

Greek Quiche

Yield: 2 servings
Total Time: 40 minutes
Ingredients:
1 cup crumbled feta cheese
4 eggs
¼ cup milk
⅓ cup chopped Kalamata olives
½ cup chopped tomatoes
1 tablespoon chopped oregano
1 tablespoon chopped basil
2 tablespoons olive oil
¼ cup chopped red onion
Salt and pepper to taste

Directions:
1. Preheat your air fryer to 340 degrees F.
2. In a bowl, beat the eggs with the milk. Season with some salt and pepper.
3. Stir in the olives, tomatoes, feta, onion, and herbs.
4. Grease a pie pan with the olive oil and then pour the egg mixture into the pan.
5. Place the pan in the air fryer.
6. Bake for 30 minutes.
7. Serve and enjoy!

Strawberry Vanilla Pancakes

Yield: 2 servings
Total Time: 20 minutes
Ingredients:
1 cup all-purpose flour
1 tablespoon maple syrup
2 eggs, beaten
½ cup milk
½ cup brown sugar
½ teaspoon baking powder
½ cup chopped strawberries
¾ teaspoon vanilla extract
Pinch of salt

Directions:
1. Preheat your air fryer to 390 degrees F.
2. Combine the flour, salt, and baking powder in a bowl.
3. In another bowl, whisk together the eggs, milk, vanilla, maple, and sugar.
4. Gently combine the two mixtures.
5. Fold in the strawberries.
6. Spray a baking dish with some cooking spray.
7. Pour the pancake batter into the dish and then place it in the air fryer.
8. Cook for 10 minutes.
9. Serve and enjoy!

Apricot Bread Pudding

Yield: 2 servings
Total Time: 15 minutes
Ingredients:
1 large egg
2/3 cup milk
⅓ cup buttermilk
1½ tablespoons butter
½ teaspoon vanilla extract
2 tablespoons brown sugar
¼ cup honey
4 tablespoons chopped dried apricots
2 tablespoons chopped pecans
5 bread slices, cubed
¼ teaspoon cinnamon

Directions:
1. In a bowl, beat the eggs along with the milk, buttermilk, vanilla, sugar, butter, and honey.
2. Stir in the chopped pecans and apricots.
3. Add the bread cubes to the bowl and stir well. Make sure they are completely soaked.
4. Let sit for about 10 minutes.
5. Meanwhile, preheat your air fryer to 330 degrees F.
6. Transfer the bread pudding to a baking dish and place it into the air fryer.
7. Bake for 20 minutes.
8. Sprinkle with the cinnamon and serve.

Breakfast Burrito

Yield: 2 servings
Total Time: 15 minutes
Ingredients:
2 large eggs
4 thin slices turkey or chicken
4 tablespoons bell pepper, diced
6 thin avocado slices
3 tablespoons grated mozzarella
2 tortillas
3 tablespoons salsa
Salt and pepper to taste

Directions:
1. Preheat air fryer to 360 degrees F.
2. Whisk the eggs in a bowl and add salt and pepper.
3. Place a small pan inside the basket of the air fryer. Spray the pan with a non-stick cooking spray.
4. Pour the eggs into the pan and cook for 5 minutes.
5. Carefully remove the pan from the air fryer.
6. Fill the tortillas with equal amounts of egg, turkey or chicken, bell pepper, avocado, grated cheese, and salsa. Be careful not to overstuff the tortillas.
7. Roll and firmly wrap the tortillas.
8. Place the tortillas on a tray in the air fryer.
9. Decrease the temperature to 350 degrees F and cook for 3 minutes.
10. Serve hot, with salsa on the side.

French Toast Triangles

Yield: 2 servings
Total Time: 15 minutes
Ingredients:
4 pieces of your favorite bread
2 eggs, beaten
2 tablespoons butter
1 teaspoon salt
2 teaspoons cinnamon
1 teaspoon nutmeg
Powdered sugar and syrup for serving

Directions:
1. Preheat your air fryer to 350 degrees F.
2. Beat the eggs in a bowl and add salt, cinnamon, and nutmeg.
3. Butter each side of the bread slices, and cut them diagonally, so you have four wedges for each slice. Soak each wedge in the egg mixture and arrange in the air fryer basket (you will need to cook more than one batch).
4. Cook in the air fryer for 3 minutes.
5. Flip the toast wedges over to the other side and cook for another 3 minutes.
6. Dust with powdered sugar or drizzle with syrup.

Banana and Oat Muffins

Yield: 2 servings
Total Time: 15 minutes
Ingredients:
2 tablespoons powdered sugar
2 tablespoons mashed bananas
1 teaspoon milk
2 tablespoons butter
1 teaspoon finely chopped walnuts
2 tablespoons all-purpose flour
2 tablespoons oats
¼ teaspoon baking powder

Directions:
1. Preheat your air fryer to 320 degrees F.
2. Combine the sugar, banana, milk, butter, and walnuts in a bowl.
3. In another bowl, whisk together the flour, oats, and baking powder.
4. Combine the two mixtures.
5. Grease two muffin cups and divide the batter among them.
6. Place the muffin cups in the air fryer, close it, and cook for 10 minutes.
7. Serve and enjoy!

CHAPTER THREE

Lunch Recipes

Turkey and Cheese Sandwich

Yield: 2 servings
Total Time: 15 minutes
Ingredients:
1½ tablespoons butter, melted
4 bread slices
2/3 cup cooked and shredded turkey meat
2 teaspoons mayonnaise
2 pinches of red pepper flakes
4 mozzarella slices
½ cup shredded cabbage
1 teaspoon balsamic vinegar
2 teaspoons olive oil
Salt and pepper to taste
½ cup shredded cheddar cheese

Directions:
1. Preheat your air fryer to 350 degrees F.
2. Brush the inside of the bread slices with the butter.
3. Divide the turkey between two bread slices and top with mayo and pepper flakes.
4. Top with the mozzarella slices.
5. In a bowl, combine the cabbage, oil, and balsamic vinegar. Season with some salt and pepper to taste.
6. Divide the cabbage between the sandwiches and top with the cheddar.

7. Close the sandwiches and secure with toothpicks if desired. Place in the air fryer.

8. Bake for 7 minutes.

9. Cut in half and serve.

Sour Cream Bacon & Potato Salad

Yield: 2 servings

Total Time: 15 minutes

Ingredients:

½ pounds potatoes, boiled and cubed

4 bacon slices, chopped

¼ teaspoon garlic salt

Pinch of pepper

3 ounces sour cream

⅓ cup shredded cheddar cheese

1 teaspoon chopped parsley

Directions:

1. Preheat your air fryer to 350 degrees F.

2. In a large bowl, combine the bacon, potatoes, garlic salt, and pepper.

3. Spray a baking dish with cooking spray and then transfer the potato mixture to it.

4. Place the dish in the air fryer and bake for 7 minutes.

5. Stir in the sour cream and top with the shredded cheddar.

6. Bake for one more minute.

7. Garnish with parsley and serve.

Cheesy Eggplant Sandwich

Yield: 2 servings
Total Time: 15 minutes
Ingredients:
½ cup breadcrumbs
2 tablespoons grated parmesan cheese
½ teaspoon Italian seasoning
¼ teaspoon onion powder
¼ teaspoon garlic powder
Salt and pepper to taste
2 tablespoons milk
½ cup mayo
1 medium eggplant, sliced
¼ cup tomato sauce
4 slices Italian bread
½ cup shredded mozzarella cheese

Directions:
1. Preheat your air fryer to 400 degrees F.
2. In a shallow dish, combine the breadcrumbs, parmesan, spices, and seasonings.
3. In another bowl, whisk together the mayo and milk.
4. Dip the eggplant slices in the milk/mayo mixture and then coat with the breadcrumbs.
5. Arrange them inside the air fryer and spray with cooking spray.
6. Cook for 15 minutes, turning them over once.
7. Divide the eggplants between 2 bread slices.
8. Top with tomato sauce and mozzarella.
9. Place the other bread slices on top.
10. Serve and enjoy!

Pepperoni Pizza

Yield: 2 servings
Total Time: 15 minutes
Ingredients:
½ pound fresh pizza dough
½ cup prepared pizza sauce
¼ cup pepperoni slices or chunks
¼ cup mushrooms, sliced
¼ cup shredded mozzarella cheese
1 teaspoon dried oregano
8 muffin tins

Directions:
1. Preheat air fryer to 400 degrees F.
2. Press pizza dough into the muffin tins.
3. In a bowl, mix the pizza sauce, pepperoni, mushrooms, cheese, and oregano. Spoon into the muffin tins.
4. Cook in the air fryer for 10 minutes.

Quinoa Salad with Cheese and Prosciutto

Yield: 2 servings
Total Time: 10 minutes
Ingredients:
1 cup cooked quinoa
1 small bell pepper, chopped
1 teaspoon olive oil
¼ cup chopped olives
½ cup crumbled feta cheese
2 prosciutto slices, chopped
Salt and pepper to taste

Directions:
1. Preheat your air fryer to 350 degrees F.
2. In a bowl, combine the oil and bell pepper. Add to the air fryer and cook for 2 minutes.
3. Open the fryer, add the prosciutto, and cook for another 2 minutes.
4. Take a heatproof bowl and combine the feta, quinoa, and olives. Stir in the cooked peppers and prosciutto.
5. Place the bowl in the air fryer.
6. Cook for 2 minutes.
7. Serve and enjoy!

Beef and Cheese Egg Rolls

Yield: 2 servings
Total Time: 20 minutes
Ingredients:
½ package egg roll wrappers
1 carrot, grated
½ cup shredded mozzarella cheese
½ cup cooked ground beef
1 teaspoon olive oil
Pinch of salt
Pinch of pepper

Directions:
1. Preheat your air fryer to 370 degrees F.
2. Combine the beef, cheese, carrot, salt, and pepper in a bowl.
3. Lay out the egg roll wrappers on a clean and dry kitchen counter.
4. Divide the beef and cheese mixture between them.
5. Roll them up into egg rolls, making sure that the filling stays secured.
6. Brush the bottom of the air fryer with the olive oil and arrange the egg rolls inside.
7. Bake for 13 minutes.
8. Serve and enjoy!

Tomato and Mozzarella Bruschetta

Yield: 2 servings
Total Time: 10 minutes
Ingredients:
3 bread slices, halved
6 mozzarella slices
6 tomato slices
1 tablespoon chopped basil
1½ tablespoons olive oil
Salt and pepper to taste

Directions:
1. Preheat your air fryer to 370 degrees F.
2. Place the bread slices in the basket and bake for 3 minutes.
3. Top each bread halve with a tomato slice, then place a mozzarella slice on top.
4. Return to the air fryer and bake for 2 more minutes.
5. Drizzle with the olive oil, sprinkle with basil, and then season with some salt and pepper.
6. Serve and enjoy!

Lunch Sausage Patties

Yield: 2 servings
Total Time: 20 minutes
Ingredients:
½ pound ground Italian sausage
3 tablespoons breadcrumbs
1 small egg, beaten
½ teaspoon red pepper flakes
¼ teaspoon garlic powder
¼ teaspoon onion powder
Salt and pepper to taste

Directions:
1. Preheat your air fryer to 350 degrees F.
2. Place all ingredients in a bowl and mix with your hands until well incorporated.
3. Form 2 large or 4 small patties out of the mixture.
4. Spray the bottom of the air fryer with some cooking spray and arrange the patties inside.
5. Bake for 15 minutes.
6. Serve with your favorite sauce.
7. Enjoy!

Cabbage and Carrot Spring Rolls

Yield: 2 servings
Total Time: 15 minutes
Ingredients:
¼ head cabbage, shredded
1 carrot, grated
½ teaspoon sesame oil
½ teaspoon sesame seeds
½ teaspoon olive oil
½ teaspoon minced ginger
½ teaspoon soy sauce
½ teaspoon minced garlic
½ package spring roll wrappers

Directions:
1. Preheat your air fryer to 370 degrees F.
2. Place everything, except the wrappers, in a bowl.
3. Stir to combine well.
4. Lay the spring roll wrappers out on a clean, dry flat surface.
5. Divide the filling among them.
6. Roll them up into spring rolls, keeping the filling secured.
7. Place the rolls on a lined baking sheet that can fit into the air fryer.
8. Fry for 5 minutes.
9. Serve and enjoy!

Baked Eggs and Tomatoes

Yield: 2 servings
Total Time: 15 minutes
Ingredients:
1 tomato, sliced
2 eggs
2 tablespoons whole milk or cream
3 tablespoons cheddar cheese, grated
Salt and pepper to taste
Optional: 1 teaspoon of your favorite herbs

Directions:
1. Heat the air fryer to 360 degrees F.
2. Divide the sliced tomato between 2 ramekins.
3. Add salt, pepper, and any herbs of your choice.
4. In a bowl, whisk the eggs and milk together.
5. Transfer the egg mixture to the 2 ramekins. Top with the grated cheese.
6. Place the ramekins in the basket of the air fryer. Cook for 10 minutes.
7. Serve with hot sauce, sour cream, or salsa.

CHAPTER FOUR

Snacks and Appetizers

Chili Lime Corn

Yield: 2 servings
Total Time: 20 minutes
Ingredients:
2 corn cobs
Juice of 1 lime
1 teaspoon chopped cilantro
1 teaspoon chili powder
2 ounces feta cheese, crumbled

Directions:
1. Preheat your air fryer to 370 degrees F.
2. Place the feta in the freezer while preparing everything else.
3. Peel the corn and then remove the silk carefully.
4. Grease the bottom of the air fryer with cooking spray and then place the corn inside.
5. Bake for 15 minutes.
6. In a bowl, combine the lime juice, cilantro, and chili.
7. Drizzle over the corn.
8. Grate the frozen feta over.
9. Serve and enjoy!

Pancake Batter Onion Rings

Yield: 2 servings
Total Time: 20 minutes
Ingredients:
1 cup pancake mix
1 cup water
¼ teaspoon salt
1 large sweet onion, sliced into rings
½ cup panko breadcrumbs

Directions:
1. Preheat your air fryer to 370 degrees F.
2. In a bowl, whisk together the water and pancake mix. Stir in the salt.
3. Line a baking sheet that can fit into the air fryer with parchment paper.
4. Dip the onion rings in the pancake batter.
5. In a shallow dish, press the onion rings into the breadcrumbs.
6. Arrange on the lined baking sheet.
7. Place the sheet in the air fryer and bake for 10 minutes.
8. Serve and enjoy!

Mozzarella Sticks

Yield: 2 servings
Total Time: 40 minutes
Ingredients:
4 ounces mozzarella cheese
½ cup breadcrumbs
1 small egg
Pinch of salt
½ teaspoon garlic powder

Directions:
1. Beat the egg with the salt and garlic powder.
2. Cut the mozzarella into sticks and dip them in the egg mixture.
3. In a shallow dish, press the sticks into the breadcrumbs.
4. Arrange on a lined baking sheet and place in the freezer for at least 20 minutes.
5. Meanwhile, preheat your air fryer to 370 degrees F.
6. Grease the bottom of the air fryer with some cooking spray and arrange the mozzarella sticks inside.
7. Fry for 5 minutes. Turn them over at least once to ensure an even golden color.
8. Serve and enjoy!

Eggplant Strips

Yield: 2 servings
Total Time: 20 minutes
Ingredients:
1 medium eggplant
1 tablespoon olive oil
¼ cup bread crumbs
2 tablespoons grated parmesan cheese
½ tablespoon garlic salt
½ tablespoon dried parsley
½ tablespoon dried oregano
Salt and pepper to taste
2 tablespoons prepared spicy mayo

Directions:
1. Preheat the air fryer to 400 degrees F.
2. Wash the eggplant and pat dry. Cut it in half lengthwise and then slice into strips. Cut the long strips in half. Sprinkle with salt and pepper and drizzle with olive oil. Toss to ensure all the strips are coated.
3. In a bowl, combine the bread crumbs, cheese, and spices.
4. Add the eggplant strips to the mixture, coating.
5. Cook in the fryer for 5 minutes, and give the basket a shake.
6. Cook for another 3 minutes.
7. Serve with spicy mayo or your favorite dipping sauce.

Smoked Paprika Pickles

Yield: 2 servings
Total Time: 15 minutes
Ingredients:
1 egg
1 teaspoon smoked paprika
8 pickles
4 tablespoons all-purpose flour
1 tablespoon olive oil
¼ teaspoon garlic salt
½ cup panko breadcrumbs

Directions:
1. Preheat your air fryer to 350 degrees F.
2. Cut the pickles in half lengthwise, then pat them dry with paper towels.
3. In a bowl, combine the paprika, garlic salt, and flour.
4. In another bowl, beat the egg.
5. Line a baking sheet with a piece of parchment paper.
6. Dip the pickles in egg first, then coat with the flour mixture.
7. Place them on the baking sheet and into the air fryer.
8. Fry for 10 minutes.
9. Serve and enjoy!

Air Fried French Fries

Yield: 2 servings
Total Time: 30 minutes
Ingredients:
2/3 pound potatoes, peeled and cut into sticks
2 tablespoons olive oil
¼ teaspoon paprika
½ teaspoon garlic salt
2 tablespoons grated parmesan cheese
Pinch of pepper
Pinch of turmeric powder

Directions:
1. Preheat your air fryer to 390 degrees F.
2. Place the potatoes in a bowl. Add the olive oil, parmesan, and seasonings. Toss well to combine.
3. Transfer the seasoned potatoes to the air fryer basket.
4. Fry for 20 minutes.
5. Serve and enjoy!

Caulicheese Tater Tots

Yield: 2 servings
Total Time: 25 minutes
Ingredients:
½ pound cauliflower florets, steamed
1 small egg, beaten
¼ onion, diced
¼ cup panko breadcrumbs
¼ teaspoon garlic powder
¼ teaspoon Italian seasoning
Salt and pepper to taste

Directions:
1. Preheat your air fryer to 370 degrees F.
2. Place the cauliflower, garlic powder, Italian seasoning, and salt and pepper in a bowl.
3. Mix with your hands while squeezing until well combined.
4. Make small balls out of the mixture.
5. Dip them in egg first and then coat with the breadcrumbs.
6. Spray the bottom of your air fryer with cooking spray and arrange the tater tots inside.
7. Fry for 15 minutes.
8. Serve and enjoy!

Battered Asparagus

Yield: 2 servings
Total Time: 20 minutes
Ingredients:
⅓ pound asparagus spears, halved
⅓ cup breadcrumbs
¼ cup grated parmesan cheese
1 small egg, beaten
¼ cup flour
¼ teaspoon smoked paprika

Directions:
1. Preheat your air fryer to 370 degrees F.
2. In a bowl, combine the parmesan cheese, breadcrumbs, and paprika.
3. Dip the asparagus in flour, then into the egg, and then coat with the parmesan and breadcrumb mixture.
4. Grease the bottom of your air fryer with cooking spray and arrange the battered asparagus inside.
5. Air fry for 10 minutes.
6. Serve and enjoy!

Ham and Cheese Pinwheels

Yield: 2 servings
Total Time: 50 minutes
Ingredients:
⅓ sheet puff pastry
4 ham slices
2 teaspoons Dijon mustard
½ cup grated cheddar cheese

Directions:
1. Roll out the pastry on a clean, lightly floured kitchen counter.
2. Brush the mustard over the pastry and arrange the ham slices over the mustard.
3. Top with the grated cheese.
4. Roll up the pastry into a log, starting from the shorter edge.
5. Wrap the log in plastic wrap and place it in the freezer for 30 minutes.
6. Meanwhile, preheat your air fryer to 370 degrees F.
7. Unwrap the log and cut it into slices.
8. Line a baking sheet with a piece of parchment paper and arrange the pinwheels on top.
9. Place in the air fryer and cook for 10 minutes.
10. Serve and enjoy!

CHAPTER FIVE

Poultry

Honey and Garlic Chicken Wings

Yield: 2 servings
Total Time: 20 minutes
Ingredients:
8 chicken wings
⅓ cup cornstarch
2 tablespoons butter, melted
2 garlic cloves, minced
2 tablespoons honey
¼ teaspoon onion powder
Salt and pepper to taste

Directions:
1. Preheat your air fryer to 400 degrees F.
2. Wash the wings well, pat them dry with paper towels, and then place them in a bowl.
3. Add the cornstarch and coat the wings well.
4. Spray the bottom of the air fryer with cooking spray and place the chicken wings inside.
5. Cook for 10 minutes.
6. Take the basket out and shake or turn the wings to ensure even heating. Cook for another 10 minutes.
7. Meanwhile, whisk together the butter, honey, garlic, onion powder, and some salt and pepper.
8. Pour the wings into a bowl and cover with the sauce.
9. Serve and enjoy!

Chicken' Stir Fry'

Yield: 2 servings
Total Time: 25 minutes
Ingredients:
½ bell pepper, cut into strips
1 carrot, sliced
2 boneless and skinless chicken breasts, chopped
½ cup peas
½ cup broccoli florets
1 green onion, sliced

Sauce:
½ tablespoon brown sugar
1 teaspoon sriracha
1½ tablespoons soy sauce
1 teaspoon cornstarch
1 teaspoon minced garlic
1 teaspoon minced ginger
1 tablespoon oyster sauce
½ tablespoon red wine vinegar

Directions:
1. Preheat your air fryer to 370 degrees F.
2. In a bowl, whisk together the sauce ingredients.
3. Place the chicken, carrots, and bell pepper in the bowl.
4. Stir to combine well.
5. Line a baking dish with parchment paper and arrange the coated chicken and veggies on it.
6. Place the dish in the air fryer and cook for 7 minutes.
7. Add the remaining veggies and cook for 8 more minutes.
8. Serve and enjoy!

Maple-Glazed Turkey Breasts

Yield: 2 servings
Total Time: 20 minutes
Ingredients:
¾ pound turkey breast
1 teaspoon olive oil
¼ teaspoon sage
¼ teaspoon thyme
¼ teaspoon smoked paprika
Salt and pepper to taste
1 tablespoon butter
1 tablespoon Dijon mustard
2 tablespoons maple syrup

Directions:
1. Preheat your air fryer to 350 degrees F.
2. Brush the turkey with the olive oil.
3. In a small bowl, combine the herbs, spices, and salt, and rub the mixture into the meat.
4. Place the turkey inside the air fryer basket and cook for 25 minutes, turning it over once.
5. Meanwhile, whisk together the butter, Dijon, and maple syrup.
6. When the time is up, open the fryer, and brush the maple glaze over the turkey.
7. Cook for another 5 minutes.
8. Let sit for 5 minutes before slicing.
9. Serve and enjoy!

Lemon and Rosemary Chicken

Yield: 2 servings
Total Time: 60 minutes
Ingredients:
1 tablespoon oyster sauce
½ tablespoon olive oil
1 tablespoon soy sauce
1 teaspoon grated ginger
2 tablespoons brown sugar
2 rosemary sprigs, chopped
2 chicken breasts
½ lemon, sliced

Directions:
1. In a bowl, whisk together the olive oil, soy sauce, ginger, brown sugar, oyster sauce, and rosemary.
2. Add the chicken and stir to coat well.
3. Place in the fridge for 1 hour.
4. Preheat your air fryer to 370 degrees F.
5. Transfer the chicken to the air fryer and cook for 10 minutes.
6. Open the fryer and arrange the lemon slices on top.
7. Cook for 8 more minutes.
8. Slice the chicken breast and serve.

Pickle-Brined Chicken Legs

Yield: 2 servings
Total Time: 3 hours 30 minutes
Ingredients:
2 chicken legs, cut into drumsticks and thighs
½ of the pickle juice from a 24-ounce pickle jar
1 egg
¼ teaspoon salt
¼ teaspoon paprika
¼ teaspoon garlic powder
¼ cup flour
½ cup breadcrumbs

Directions:
1. Place the chicken legs in a bowl and pour the pickle juice over.
2. Cover and place in the fridge for 3 hours.
3. Preheat your air fryer to 370 degrees F.
4. Whisk the egg with the spices in a bowl.
5. Dip the chicken legs in flour first, then in egg mixture, then coat with breadcrumbs.
6. Spray the bottom of the air fryer with cooking spray and place the battered chicken legs inside.
7. Fry for 20 minutes, flipping over once halfway through.
8. Serve and enjoy!

Crunchy Turkey

Yield: 2 servings
Total Time: 25 minutes
Ingredients:
¾ pound turkey breast
½ salted butter Stick, melted
Pinch of pepper
1 cup breadcrumbs
¼ teaspoon garlic salt
¼ teaspoon paprika

Directions:
1. Preheat your air fryer to 370 degrees F.
2. Combine the butter and pepper, and brush the mixture over the turkey.
3. In a shallow dish, combine the breadcrumbs, garlic salt, and paprika.
4. Coat the turkey well with the mixture.
5. Grease the bottom of the air fryer with some cooking spray and place the turkey inside.
6. Cook for 15 minutes.
7. Flip the turkey over and cook for another 8 minutes.
8. Serve and enjoy!

Air Fried Cordon Bleu

Yield: 2 servings
Total Time: 75 minutes
Ingredients:
1 large chicken breast
1 tablespoon cream cheese
¼ teaspoon garlic powder
Salt and pepper to taste
1 ham slice
1 slice of swiss cheese
1 egg, beaten
2 ounces breadcrumbs
¼ teaspoon thyme

Directions:
1. Use a sharp knife to cut a slit in the middle of the chicken breast, but not all the way through.
2. Pound with a meat tenderizer mallet to flatten it a bit.
3. Season chicken with salt and pepper.
4. Brush the cream cheese into the opening and sprinkle with the garlic powder.
5. Place the ham and cheese on top of the cream cheese.
6. Press to seal the opening and keep the stuffing inside.
7. Wrap in a plastic wrap and place in the fridge for 30 minutes.
8. Meanwhile, preheat your air fryer to 370 degrees F and combine the breadcrumbs and thyme.
9. Dip the chicken in egg first, then in breadcrumbs.
10. Spray the bottom of the air fryer with some cooking spray and place the Cordon Bleu inside.
11. Cook for 30 minutes, turning over once.
12. Serve and enjoy!

Coconut-Crusted Turkey Breast

Yield: 2 servings
Total Time: 25 minutes
Ingredients:
¼ cups coconut flakes
¾ pound turkey breast, cut in half
¼ cup cornstarch
Salt and pepper to taste
1 egg, beaten

Directions:
1. Preheat your air fryer to 350 degrees F.
2. In a bowl, combine the cornstarch with salt and pepper.
3. Dip the turkey in cornstarch first, then in egg, and finally coat it with coconut.
4. Grease the bottom of the air fryer with cooking spray and place the coated turkey inside.
5. Cook for 10 minutes.
6. Flip over and cook for another 8 minutes.
7. Serve and enjoy!

Fried Chicken Sandwich

Yield: 2 servings
Total Time: 20 minutes
Ingredients:
2 chicken breasts, boneless and skinless
2 large eggs
½ cup whole milk
1 cup flour
2 tablespoons sugar
½ teaspoon garlic powder
2 tablespoons olive oil
2 hamburger buns
Salt and pepper to taste

Directions:
1. Heat the air fry to 350 degrees F.
2. Place the chicken breasts in a plastic bag and use a mallet to pound the meat to a ½-inch thickness.
3. Cut the chicken into several large pieces.
4. Whisk the eggs and milk in a bowl.
5. In another bowl, stir the flour with the sugar, garlic powder, salt, and pepper.
6. Dip the chicken pieces in the egg mixture, then coat them with the flour mixture.
7. Spray the bottom of the air fryer with a non-stick cooking spray. Cook chicken for 5 minutes.
8. Flip the chicken and cook another 6 minutes.
9. Increase the heat to 390 degrees F and cook for 2 more minutes.
10. Toast the hamburger buns and assemble the sandwiches.
11. If desired, add mayonnaise and pickles.

Easy Buffalo Ranch Chicken Wings

Yield: 2 servings
Total Time: 25 minutes
Ingredients:
1 pound chicken wings, drums, and flats
¼ cup wing sauce
¼ cup ranch dressing

Directions:
1. Preheat your air fryer to 375 degrees F.
2. Put the wings in the fryer basket and cook for 15 minutes.
3. Take the basket out and shake or turn the wings to ensure even heating. Cook for another 10 minutes.
4. Pour into a bowl and cover with wing sauce and ranch dressing.

CHAPTER SIX

Meats

Air Fried Chili

Yield: 2 servings
Total Time: 50 minutes
Ingredients:
1 tablespoon olive oil
1 bell pepper, diced
1 garlic clove, minced
¼ onion, diced
½ pound ground beef
1 teaspoon chili powder
½ can diced tomatoes
¾ cup vegetable broth
½ teaspoon parsley
½ can cannellini beans
Salt and pepper to taste

Directions:
1. Preheat your air fryer to 350 degrees F.
2. In a heatproof dish, combine the oil, pepper, garlic, and onion.
3. Place the dish in the air fryer and cook for 5 minutes.
4. Open the fryer and add beef to the dish. Stir to combine.
5. Cook for 6 more minutes.
6. Stir in the tomatoes, broth, chili powder, and parsley, and cook for 20 minutes.
7. Add the beans and some salt and pepper. Stir to combine and cook for another 10 minutes.
8. Serve and enjoy!

Worcestershire Meatloaf

Yield: 2 servings
Total Time: 35 minutes
Ingredients:
¼ onion, diced
¾ pound ground beef
¼ cup breadcrumbs
1 tablespoon ketchup
1 tablespoon Worcestershire sauce
1 teaspoon sugar
1 teaspoon Italian seasoning
¼ teaspoon garlic salt
Pinch of pepper
¼ teaspoon paprika

Directions:
1. Preheat your air fryer to 350 degrees F.
2. Place all of the ingredients in a large bowl.
3. Mix with your hand until fully incorporated.
4. Grease a loaf pan with some cooking spray or oil. Press the beef mixture into it.
5. Place the loaf pan in the air fryer.
6. Cook for 25 minutes.
7. Serve and enjoy!

Simple Flank Steak

Yield: 2 servings
Total Time: 25 minutes
Ingredients:
¾ pounds flank steak
1½ teaspoons steak rub
1 tablespoon olive oil

Directions:
1. Preheat your air fryer to 400 degrees F.
2. Combine the steak rub and olive oil, and rub the mixture into the meat.
3. Place the steak in the air fryer.
4. Cook for 10 minutes, flip over and cook for 7 more minutes.
5. Let the steak sit for 5 minutes before slicing.
6. Serve and enjoy!

The Ultimate Burgers

Yield: 2 servings
Total Time: 20 minutes
Ingredients:
½ pound ground beef
¼ teaspoon onion powder
¼ teaspoon garlic powder
½ tablespoon Worcestershire sauce
½ teaspoon dried parsley
¼ teaspoon salt
¼ teaspoon pepper
2 tablespoons breadcrumbs

Directions:
1. Preheat your air fryer to 370 degrees F.
2. In a bowl, place all of the ingredients.
3. Mix well with your hand until the mixture is fully incorporated.
4. Shape into 2 burger patties.
5. Grease the bottom of the air fryer with some cooking spray and add the burger patties inside.
6. Cook for 15 minutes, flipping over once.
7. Serve and enjoy!

Roasted Pork Belly

Yield: 2 servings
Total Time: 3 hours 10 minutes
Ingredients:
¾ pound pork belly
½ teaspoon five-spice powder
¼ teaspoon onion powder
¼ teaspoon white pepper
¼ teaspoon garlic salt

Directions:
1. Blanch the pork belly by placing it in a bowl and covering it with boiling water. Let sit for 2 minutes.
2. Drain the water and allow the pork to air dry for about 2 hours.
3. Meanwhile, preheat your air fryer to 330 degrees F.
4. If the pork is still wet in some places, pat it dry with paper towels.
5. With a fork, pierce the meat a couple of times.
6. In a small bowl, combine the seasonings and rub them into the meat.
7. Grease the bottom of the air fryer with cooking spray and place the pork belly inside.
8. Cook for 30 minutes.
9. Open the fryer, flip the pork over, and cook for another 30 minutes.
10. Serve and enjoy!

Gingery Pork Ribs

Yield: 2 servings
Total Time: 5 hours
Ingredients:
1 pound pork ribs
1 tablespoon minced ginger
1 tablespoon hoisin sauce
1 teaspoon minced garlic
1 tablespoon soy sauce
1 tablespoon sesame oil
½ tablespoon honey
Pinch of salt
Pinch of pepper

Directions:
1. Place the pork ribs in a bowl.
2. Whisk together the remaining ingredients in a smaller bowl and pour the mixture over the ribs.
3. Coat the ribs well and cover the bowl. Place in the fridge for 4 hours.
4. Preheat your air fryer to 370 degrees F.
5. Transfer the marinated pork ribs to the air fryer's basket, but reserve the marinade.
6. Cook for 40 minutes.
7. Open the lid, brush the marinade over the ribs, and cook for another 10 minutes, or until sticky.
8. Serve and enjoy!

Apple Pork Chops

Yield: 2 servings
Total Time: 45 minutes
Ingredients:
2 pork chops
1 tablespoon olive oil
1 tablespoon apple cider vinegar
1 apple, peeled and sliced
½ red onion, sliced
Pinch of brown sugar
¼ teaspoon dried rosemary
Salt and pepper to taste

Directions:
1. Preheat your air fryer to 350 degrees F.
2. In a heatproof dish, combine the apples, onion, sugar, rosemary, and half of the oil and vinegar.
3. Air fry for 4 minutes.
4. Whisk the remaining vinegar and oil with salt and pepper and brush over the pork chops.
5. Place the pork chops inside the dish.
6. Close the air fryer and cook for another 15 minutes.
7. Serve the pork chops with the apple toppings.
8. Enjoy!

Lamb Kebab

Yield: 2 servings
Total Time: 40 minutes
Ingredients:
½ pound ground lamb
¼ teaspoon paprika
¼ teaspoon parsley
¼ teaspoon garlic powder
Pinch of salt
Pinch of pepper
2 tablespoons breadcrumbs
1 teaspoon chopped mint
¼ teaspoon cumin

Directions:
1. Preheat your air fryer to 370 degrees F.
2. Place all of the ingredients in a bowl.
3. Mix with your hands until you combine the mixture well.
4. Shape the lamb mixture around the skewers.
5. Spray the bottom of the air fryer with cooking spray and place the lamb kebabs inside.
6. Cook for 15 minutes.
7. Serve and enjoy!

Cheeseburger with Everything

Yield: 2 servings
Total Time: 15 minutes
Ingredients:
1 pound ground beef
2 slices Swiss or American cheese
4 bacon strips (optional)
2 hamburger buns
4 onion slices
4 tomato slices
Lettuce leaves
Condiments

Directions:
1. Heat the air fryer to 360 degrees F.
2. Shape the ground beef into 2 patties.
3. Place patties and bacon into the air fryer basket. Cook for 8 minutes.
4. Top the hamburger patties with cheese and onions.
5. Place the sliced buns on top of the burgers.
6. Continue cooking for 3 minutes.
7. Add tomato slices, lettuce, and desired condiments.

Pigs in Blankets

Yield: 2 servings
Total Time: 15 minutes
Ingredients:
20 mini hot dogs or Vienna sausages
10 Strips of refrigerated puff pastry, cut in half
¼ cup barbeque sauce

Directions:
1. Preheat your air fryer to 390 degrees F.
2. Spread each strip of pastry with barbeque sauce.
3. Wrap the strips of pastry around the hot dogs securely.
4. Place them in the air fryer basket and cook for 10 minutes (two batches may be necessary).
5. Serve with extra barbeque sauce.

CHAPTER SEVEN

Fish and Seafood

Lemon Pepper Tilapia

Yield: 2 servings
Total Time: 15 minutes
Ingredients:
2 tilapia fillets
2 tablespoons flour
Pinch of salt
¼ teaspoon pepper
2 tablespoons instant potato flakes
½ cup breadcrumbs
1 tablespoon lemon juice
¼ teaspoon lemon pepper
1 egg, beaten

Directions:
1. Preheat your air fryer to 370 degrees F.
2. In a shallow dish, combine the flour, salt, and pepper.
3. In another dish, combine the potato flakes, breadcrumbs, lemon juice, and lemon pepper.
4. Dip the tilapia in flour first, then in egg, and coat it with the breadcrumb mixture at the end.
5. Spray a baking dish with cooking spray and place the tilapia fillets on it.
6. Place dish in the air fryer and cook for 10 minutes.
7. Serve and enjoy!

Soy Sauce Salmon

Yield: 2 servings
Total Time: 15 minutes
Ingredients:
2 salmon fillets
2 tablespoons soy sauce
¼ teaspoon garlic salt
Pinch of pepper

Directions:
1. Preheat your air fryer to 350 degrees F.
2. In a bowl, whisk together the soy sauce, garlic salt, and pepper.
3. Brush the mixture over the salmon fillets.
4. Line a baking dish with a piece of parchment paper and place the fillets onto it.
5. Place the baking dish in the air fryer.
6. Air fry for 10 minutes.
7. Serve and enjoy!

Chili Tuna Cakes

Yield: 2 servings
Total Time: 50 minutes
Ingredients:
½ onion, diced
5 ounces canned tuna, drained
¼ cup flour
2 eggs
½ cup milk
1 teaspoon lime juice
1 teaspoon paprika
2 teaspoons chili powder
¼ teaspoon garlic powder
Salt to taste

Directions:
1. Place all of the ingredients in a bowl.
2. Mix well until fully incorporated.
3. Shape the mixture into 2 patties and place them on a lined baking sheet.
4. Refrigerate for 30 minutes.
5. Meanwhile, preheat your air fryer to 350 degrees F.
6. Spray the bottom of the air fryer with some cooking spray. Place the patties in the air fryer and cook for about 6 minutes per side.
7. Serve and enjoy!

Coconut Shrimp

Yield: 2 servings
Total Time: 30 minutes
Ingredients:
½ cup shredded coconut
½ teaspoon cayenne pepper
½ cup breadcrumbs
Salt and pepper to taste
8 large shrimps
8 ounces coconut milk
½ cup orange jam
1 tablespoon honey
1 teaspoon Dijon mustard

Directions:
1. Preheat your air fryer to 350 degrees F.
2. In a shallow dish, combine the coconut, cayenne, breadcrumbs, and some salt and pepper.
3. Dip the shrimp in coconut milk first and then coat with the breadcrumb mixture.
4. Coat the air fryer basket with a non-stick cooking spray. Place shrimps in the basket.
5. Cook for 10 minutes.
6. Meanwhile, whisk together the remaining ingredients.
7. Serve the shrimp with the orange jam dipping sauce.
8. Enjoy!

Popcorn Shrimp

Yield: 2 servings
Total Time: 25 minutes
Ingredients:
24 medium uncooked white shrimps
1 cup flour
1 cup panko breadcrumbs
1 cup dried, unsweetened coconut
1 tablespoon cornstarch
4 egg whites

Directions:
1. Preheat air fryer to 350 degrees F.
2. Rinse and dry shrimp.
3. In two separate bowls, mix the breadcrumbs and the coconut and then the flour and the cornstarch.
4. Dip one shrimp at a time into the flour mixture, the egg whites, and then the coconut.
5. Place in the basket and cook for 10 minutes. Check the shrimp and turn or shake.
6. Cook another 5 minutes.

Cajun Shrimp

Yield: 2 servings
Total Time: 15 minutes
Ingredients:
16 large shrimps, peeled and deveined
1 tablespoon celery salt
¼ teaspoon cayenne pepper
¼ teaspoon paprika
Dash of dry mustard
Dash of cinnamon
Salt and pepper to taste
1 tablespoon olive oil

Directions:
1. Preheat air fryer to 380 degrees F.
2. In a bowl, mix all of the spices and the oil.
3. Coat the shrimp thoroughly with the spice mix.
4. Cook in the air fryer for 6 minutes.
5. Serve with rice.

Crunchy Haddock

Yield: 2 servings
Total Time: 20 minutes
Ingredients:
2 haddock fillets
1 tablespoon olive oil
1 small egg, beaten
2 biscuits, crumbled
2 tablespoons sesame seeds
2 tablespoons flour
¼ teaspoon rosemary
¼ teaspoon lemon pepper
¼ teaspoon garlic salt

Directions:
1. Preheat your air fryer to 390 degrees F.
2. In a bowl, combine the flour, pepper, and salt.
3. In another bowl, combine the biscuit crumbs, sesame seeds, and rosemary.
4. Dip the haddock fillets in the flour mixture first, then in the egg, and finally coat with the sesame mixture.
5. Arrange a piece of parchment paper at the bottom of the air fryer.
6. Place the haddock onto the paper. Cook for 8 minutes.
7. Open the fryer, flip the fillets over, and cook for another 4 minutes.
8. Serve and enjoy!

Dijon and Almond Salmon

Yield: 2 servings
Total Time: 15 minutes
Ingredients:
2 salmon fillets
2 tablespoons Dijon mustard
⅓ cup slivered almonds
¼ teaspoon garlic powder
Pinch of pepper
1 teaspoon lemon juice

Directions:
1. Preheat your air fryer to 350 degrees F.
2. In a bowl, combine the mustard, lemon juice, garlic powder, and pepper.
3. Brush the mixture over the salmon fillets.
4. Coat the salmon with the slivered almond.
5. Arrange a piece of parchment paper at the bottom of the air fryer.
6. Place the salmon on the paper and air fry for 10 minutes.
7. Serve and enjoy!

Salmon and Potato Patties

Yield: 2 servings
Total Time: 1 hour 15 minutes
Ingredients:
5 ounces canned salmon, drained
1 teaspoon chopped capers
7 ounces boiled and mashed potatoes
¼ teaspoon lemon zest
1½ tablespoons flour
1 teaspoon olive oil

Directions:
1. Preheat your air fryer to 370 degrees F.
2. Place all ingredients, except the flour and oil, in a bowl.
3. Mix well until fully combined. Shape the mixture into 4 small patties.
4. Dust the patties with the flour and place on a lined baking dish.
5. Refrigerate for 1 hour.
6. Brush the oil over the bottom of the air fryer and place the patties inside.
7. Cook for 7 minutes.
8. Serve and enjoy!

Parmesan-Crusted Mackerel

Yield: 2 servings
Total Time: 15 minutes
Ingredients:
2 mackerel fillets
⅓ cup grated parmesan cheese
1 teaspoon paprika
¼ teaspoon dried parsley
Pinch of garlic salt
Pinch of pepper
2 teaspoons olive oil

Directions:
1. Preheat your air fryer to 350 degrees F.
2. In a bowl, combine the parmesan, paprika, parsley, pepper, and garlic salt.
3. Brush the mackerel with the oil and then coat with the parmesan mixture.
4. Spray the bottom of the air fryer with cooking spray and place the mackerel fillets inside.
5. Cook for 5 minutes.
6. Open the lid, flip over, and cook for another 5 minutes.
7. Serve and enjoy!

Tuna Croquettes

Yield: 2 servings
Total Time: 15 minutes
Ingredients:
2 cans of tuna, drained
2 eggs, beaten
¼ cup breadcrumbs
⅓ cup vegetable oil
2 tablespoons dried parsley
Salt and pepper to taste

Directions:
1. Preheat air fryer to 390 degrees F.
2. Mix the tuna with the eggs, oil, parsley, salt, and pepper. Roll the mixture into balls and coat them with the breadcrumbs.
3. Place them in the fryer basket and cook for 8 minutes.

Lemon Dill Salmon

Yield: 2 servings
Total Time: 15 minutes
Ingredients:
2 pieces of salmon (6-8 ounces each)
2 tablespoons fresh dill
1 lemon, juiced
1 teaspoon garlic powder
Salt and pepper to taste

Directions:
1. Preheat the air fryer to 350 degrees F.
2. Rinse salmon and pat dry. Season with salt and pepper.
3. In a bowl, combine the lemon juice, dill, and garlic powder. Pour over the salmon and lightly rub the liquid into the fish.
4. Line a baking dish with a piece of parchment paper and place the salmon onto it.
5. Place the baking dish in the air fryer. Cook for 8 minutes.
6. Serve over rice or pasta or with a large salad.

CHAPTER EIGHT

Vegetables

Cabbage Steaks

Yield: 2 servings
Total Time: 25 minutes
Ingredients:
½ medium head cabbage, sliced
1 tablespoon olive oil
1 teaspoon fennel seeds
½ teaspoon salt
½ tablespoon garlic paste
Pinch of pepper

Directions:
1. Preheat your air fryer to 350 degrees F.
2. Place the oil, fennel seeds, garlic paste, salt, and pepper, in a bowl.
3. Whisk to combine and brush the cabbage slices with the mixture.
4. Grease the bottom of the air fryer with cooking spray and then arrange the cabbage steaks inside.
5. Air fry for 15 minutes.
6. Serve and enjoy!

Riced Cauliflower with Tofu

Yield: 2 servings
Total Time: 30 minutes
Ingredients:
1½ cups riced cauliflower (ground in a food processor)
½ teaspoon vinegar
¼ cup chopped broccoli
1 tablespoon soy sauce
1 teaspoon sesame oil
1 teaspoon minced ginger
¼ cup peas

Tofu:
1 tablespoon soy sauce
¼ block tofu, crumbled
2 tablespoons diced onions
½ teaspoon turmeric
½ cup diced carrots

Directions:
1. Preheat your air fryer to 370 degrees F.
2. In a bowl, place all of the tofu ingredients and stir to combine well.
3. Transfer the mixture to a baking dish and place the dish inside the air fryer.
4. Cook for 10 minutes.
5. Meanwhile, place all of the remaining ingredients in a bowl.
6. Stir to combine well.
7. Open the air fryer and add the cauliflower mixture to the baking dish.
8. Stir to combine well and close the fryer.
9. Cook for 12 more minutes.
10. Serve and enjoy!

Veggie Pizza for Two

Yield: 2 servings
Total Time: 15 minutes
Ingredients:
1 mini pre-made pizza crust
¼ cup tomato sauce
6 eggplant slices
¼ onion, sliced
6 zucchini slices
1 red bell pepper, chopped
2 tablespoons peas
2 tablespoons corn
4 cherry tomatoes, halved
½ cup shredded mozzarella cheese
¼ teaspoon oregano

Directions:
1. Preheat your air fryer to 350 degrees F.
2. Add the pizza crust to a lined baking dish.
3. Spread the tomato sauce over.
4. Top with eggplant, onion, and zucchini slices, and scatter the bell pepper, peas, and corn over it.
5. Place the cherry tomatoes on top and sprinkle with grated mozzarella and oregano.
6. Place the baking dish in the air fryer.
7. Cook for 10 minutes.
8. Serve and enjoy!

Spicy Baby Carrots

Yield: 2 servings
Total Time: 25 minutes
Ingredients:
½ pound baby carrots
¼ teaspoon cumin
¼ teaspoon onion powder
½ teaspoon chili powder
1 tablespoon olive oil
1 garlic clove, minced
2 tablespoons chopped coriander

Directions:
1. Preheat your air fryer to 370 degrees F.
2. Place the carrots in a bowl. Add cumin, onion powder, chili powder, and olive oil.
3. Toss to coat well and transfer to the air fryer.
4. Cook for 20 minutes.
5. Place on a platter.
6. In a bowl, whisk together the garlic and coriander.
7. Sprinkle the mixture over the carrots.
8. Serve and enjoy!

Roasted Vegetables

Yield: 2 servings
Total Time: 15 minutes
Ingredients:
½ cup potato, chopped
½ cup celery stalks, chopped
1 red onion, chopped
½ butternut squash, chopped
½ tablespoon fresh thyme leaves
½ tablespoon olive oil
Salt and pepper to taste

Directions:
1. Preheat the air fryer to 390 degrees F.
2. Add potatoes, celery, onion, squash, pepper, salt, and thyme to a bowl and mix until well combined.
3. Add in oil and toss.
4. Add vegetables to the air fryer basket and fry for 10 minutes.
5. Serve hot.

Buttery Cabbage with Parmesan

Yield: 2 servings
Total Time: 30 minutes
Ingredients:
¼ cabbage, cut into 2 wedges
2 tablespoons butter, melted
Salt and pepper to taste
½ cup grated parmesan cheese
½ teaspoon smoked paprika
¼ teaspoon garlic powder

Directions:
1. Preheat your air fryer to 330 degrees F.
2. Brush the cabbage with butter and season with salt and pepper.
3. In a shallow dish, combine the parmesan, paprika, and garlic powder.
4. Coat the cabbage with the mixture.
5. Place the cabbage in the air fryer basket.
6. Bake for 15 minutes, flip over, and cook for 10 more minutes.
7. Serve and enjoy!

Crunchy Zucchini

Yield: 2 servings
Total Time: 20 minutes
Ingredients:
2 small zucchini, cut lengthwise
2 tablespoons butter, melted
1 teaspoon minced garlic
¼ cup grated parmesan cheese
½ cup breadcrumbs
¼ teaspoon turmeric powder
¼ teaspoon onion powder
¼ teaspoon red pepper flakes

Directions:
1. Preheat your air fryer to 350 degrees F.
2. Combine the breadcrumbs, parmesan, and garlic in a bowl. Stir in the butter.
3. Spray a baking dish with some cooking spray. Place the zucchini inside.
4. Spread the breadcrumb mixture over the zucchini.
5. Sprinkle with the spices.
6. Place the dish in the air fryer. Bake for 13 minutes.
7. Increase the temperature to 370 degrees and cook for another 2-3 minutes.
8. Serve and enjoy!

Air-Fried Ratatouille

Yield: 2 servings
Total Time: 30 minutes
Ingredients:
3 tomatoes, sliced
2 bell peppers, sliced
1 zucchini, sliced
1 tablespoon olive oil
2 tablespoons Herb de Provence
1 teaspoon minced garlic
1 tablespoon vinegar
Salt and pepper to taste

Directions:
1. Preheat your air fryer to 390 degrees F.
2. Place all of the ingredients in a bowl. Toss carefully to combine.
3. Add the ingredients to a baking dish. Place the dish in the air fryer.
4. Cook for 15 minutes. Make sure to give the fryer a couple of good shakes.
5. Serve and enjoy!

Stuffed Portobello Mushrooms

Yield: 2 servings
Total Time: 15 minutes
Ingredients:
2 portobello mushrooms
1 tablespoon olive oil
½ green pepper, diced
½ tomato, diced
2 tablespoons diced red onion
¼ teaspoon garlic powder
¼ cup shredded mozzarella cheese
Salt and pepper to taste

Directions:
1. Preheat your air fryer to 370 degrees F.
2. Wash the mushrooms and remove their stems. Pat dry with paper towels.
3. Brush the mushrooms with the oil.
4. In a bowl, combine the pepper, tomato, onion, and garlic powder.
5. Place the mushrooms on a baking sheet, gill sides up. Divide the veggie mixture between the mushrooms and then top with the mozzarella cheese.
6. Place the mushrooms in the air fryer and bake for 8 minutes.
7. Serve and enjoy!

CHAPTER NINE

Dessert

Simple Donuts

Yield: 2 servings
Total Time: 25 minutes
Ingredients:
1¼ tablespoons butter, melted
1 ounce brown sugar
¼ cup milk
1 small egg
4 ounces self-rising flour
½ teaspoon baking powder
Pinch of cinnamon

Directions:
1. Preheat your air fryer to 350 degrees F.
2. Beat the sugar and butter in a bowl until smooth and creamy.
3. Beat in the milk and egg.
4. Gently whisk in the flour, baking powder, and cinnamon.
5. Mix with your hands until a dough-like consistency is formed.
6. Shape the mixture into 2 big donuts.
7. Line the air fryer with parchment paper and place the donuts on it.
8. Bake for 8 minutes.
9. Serve and enjoy!

Blueberry Muffins

Yield: 2 servings
Total Time: 30 minutes
Ingredients:
¼ cup flour
1 tablespoon sugar
Pinch of baking powder
Pinch of baking soda
Pinch of salt
1 tablespoon butter, melted
3 tablespoons yogurt
¼ teaspoon vanilla extract
3 tablespoons blueberries

Directions:
1. Preheat your air fryer to 350 degrees F.
2. In a bowl, combine all of the dry ingredients.
3. Whisk together the butter, yogurt, and vanilla, in another bowl.
4. Combine the two mixtures carefully and then fold in the blueberries.
5. Divide the mixture between two silicone muffin cups and place them inside the air fryer.
6. Cook for 10 minutes.
7. Serve and enjoy!

Mocha Cake

Yield: 2 servings
Total Time: 30 minutes
Ingredients:
1 egg
¼ cup sugar
¼ cup butter, softened
1 tablespoon brewed black coffee
½ teaspoon granulated instant coffee
1 teaspoon cocoa powder
¼ cup flour
1 tablespoon milk
Pinch of salt
Powdered sugar for sprinkling

Directions:
1. Preheat your air fryer to 330 degrees F.
2. Grease a small round pan with cooking spray.
3. In a bowl, beat together the egg, sugar, and butter.
4. Beat in the coffee, instant coffee, and cocoa powder.
5. Whisk in the flour, milk, and salt and make sure there are no more lumps left before pouring the batter into the prepared baking pan.
6. Place the pan in the air fryer. Cook for 15 minutes.
7. Sprinkle with powdered sugar before serving.
8. Enjoy!

Lemon-Frosted Mini Sponge Cakes

Yield: 2 servings
Total Time: 25 minutes
Ingredients:
1 small egg
2 ounces sugar
2 ounces butter, softened
2 ounces self-rising flour
¼ teaspoon vanilla extract
¼ teaspoon baking powder
¼ teaspoon lemon zest

Frosting:
1 tablespoon lemon juice
1 egg white
½ teaspoon lemon zest
1 tablespoon sugar

Directions:
1. Preheat your air fryer to 370 degrees F.
2. Place all of the ingredients for the cake in a bowl and beat with an electric mixer until well incorporated and smooth.
3. Grease two ramekins with cooking spray and divide the batter between them.
4. Place in the air fryer and bake for 10 minutes.
5. Meanwhile, prepare the frosting by whisking all of the ingredients together.
6. Brush the frosting over the cakes.
7. Serve and enjoy!

Fruit Kabobs

Yield: 2 servings
Total Time: 15 minutes
Ingredients:
½ apple, cored and cut into chunks
½ mango, cut into chunks
½ pear, cored and cut into chunks
½ orange, peeled and divided into segments
1 teaspoon honey
1 teaspoon lemon juice
Salt to taste
2 tablespoons pomegranate seeds
Skewers

Directions:
1. Preheat the air fryer to 350 degrees F.
2. In a bowl, combine the lemon juice and honey. Add the fruit pieces and coat with the mixture. Sprinkle with salt. Divide the fruit onto skewers and place in the fryer.
3. Cook for 5 minutes for a grilled flavor.
4. Put them on a plate and sprinkle with pomegranate seeds.

Chocolate Chip Cookies

Yield: 2 servings
Total Time: 30 minutes
Ingredients:
2 ounces butter, softened
1½ ounces brown sugar
3 ounces self-rising flour
1 tablespoon milk
½ tablespoon honey
2 tablespoons chocolate chips

Directions:
1. Preheat your air fryer to 350 degrees F.
2. In a bowl, beat together the sugar and butter.
3. When fluffy, beat in the flour, milk, and honey.
4. Fold in the chocolate chips.
5. Line a baking sheet with a piece of parchment paper. Spoon the batter onto the sheet, making 2 large or 4 medium cookies.
6. Place the baking sheet in the air fryer.
7. Bake for 18 minutes.
8. Serve and enjoy!

Molten Lavas

Yield: 2 servings
Total Time: 20 minutes
Ingredients:
1 egg
1¾ tablespoons sugar
1¾ ounces butter, melted
1¾ ounces dark chocolate, melted
¼ teaspoon vanilla extract
1 tablespoon self-rising flour

Directions:
1. Preheat your air fryer to 375 degrees F and grease 2 ramekins.
2. In a bowl, beat together the egg with the sugar.
3. When frothy, beat in the vanilla, butter, and chocolate.
4. Fold in the flour carefully.
5. Pour the batter into the ramekins.
6. Place the ramekins inside the air fryer.
7. Cook for 10 minutes.
8. Let cool for a few minutes before inverting onto plates.
9. Serve with a scoop of vanilla ice cream if desired.
10. Enjoy!

Peach Crumble

Yield: 2 servings
Total Time: 30 minutes
Ingredients:
2 large peaches, pitted
1 tablespoon lemon juice
¼ cup sugar
½ cup flour
Pinch of salt
2½ tablespoons cold butter
½ tablespoon water

Directions:
1. Preheat your air fryer to 390 degrees F.
2. Place the peaches in a bowl and lightly mash them with a fork. There should be chunks left.
3. Add the lemon juice and a tablespoon of the sugar to the bowl and combine.
4. Grease a small round pan and arrange the peach mixture at the bottom.
5. In another bowl, combine the flour, sugar, and salt.
6. Add the butter and water.
7. Rub the butter into the flour with your fingers until a crumbly mixture forms.
8. Spread the crumbly mixture all over the peaches.
9. Place in the air fryer and bake for 20 minutes.
10. Serve and enjoy!

Chocolate-Filled Oat Cookies

Yield: 2 servings
Total Time: 30 minutes
Ingredients:
3 ounces flour
¼ teaspoon vanilla extract
¼ cup oats
2 tablespoons coconut flakes
1 small egg, beaten
1½ ounces sugar

Filling:
1 ounce dark chocolate, melted
2 ounces icing sugar
½ tablespoon butter
¼ teaspoon vanilla extract

Directions:
1. Preheat your air fryer to 380 degrees F.
2. In a bowl, beat all of the ingredients for the cookies (except the flour) with an electric mixer.
3. When the mixture becomes smooth, fold in the flour gently.
4. Line a baking sheet with parchment paper. Spoon the batter onto the sheet, making 4 cookies.
5. Place the baking sheet in the air fryer and cook for 18 minutes.
6. Meanwhile, beat all of the fillings together in a bowl.
7. Spread the filling on 2 of the cookies.
8. Top with the other 2 cookies.
9. Serve and enjoy!

Baked Pears

Yield: 2 servings
Total Time: 30 minutes
Ingredients:
2 pears
2 tablespoons raisins
2 tablespoons milk
1 tablespoon cinnamon
2 sheets fresh puff pastry dough (ready to use)

Directions:
1. Preheat air fryer to 350 degrees F.
2. Peel and core the pears. Slice them in half and scoop out some extra fruit to make a small hole on each side. Mix the fruit with the raisins and the cinnamon. Fill the holes in 2 of the pear halves with that mixture.
3. Place one pear half on a sheet of pastry and cover it with the corresponding (and empty) pear half, so it looks like one whole pear again. Wrap in the pastry and tuck in or fold the ends. Brush with milk. Do the same thing with the other pear halves.
4. Cook in the air fryer for 20 minutes.

Conclusion

Now, throw away your apron and surprise your loved one with some healthy and crunchy delights from the air fryer. I promise you, with these yummy recipes, dinner for two will never be the same.

Finally, I want to thank you for reading my book. If you enjoyed the book, please share your thoughts and post a review on the book retailer's website. It would be greatly appreciated!

Best wishes,

Melanie Bennet